The
FENDER GUITAR

KEN ACHARD

G118

A Guitar Magazine project
© Copyright 1977 by
MUSICAL NEW SERVICES LTD., 20 Denmark Street, London WC2H 8NE

Dedication

This work is dedicated to Leo Fender, who has done more than any one man for the electric guitar, to George Clinton, who suggested I write it, and to a long suffering wife Lin. It is also dedicated to you, dear reader, in the hope that it gives pleasure and information on one maker amongst many in the fascinating world of the guitar.

1st Print August 1977
2nd Print December 1977
3rd Print February 1978

The
FENDER GUITAR

KEN ACHARD

Contents	Page

ACKNOWLEDGEMENTS

My special thanks are due to CBS Musical Instruments, and David Gupton for their permission to reproduce Fender publicity material, and their gratefully received assistance and information. Thanks too to Tom Walker of Music Man Inc. for confirming historical authenticity, and Guitar Magazine for various photographs. A big debt of gratitude is due to Seymour Duncan Guitar Research & Repair for providing pictures and information of many interesting and rare instruments. Thank you Robert Johnson and Sid Bishop for being mates and sharing my interests in American guitars, and George Clinton for his help, assistance, guidance and arm-twisting! To all my friends who share, foster and encourage me.

INTRODUCTION

Fender has become known as one of the big names in the musical instrument world, because it grew up with, and was an important part of that tremendous evolution of popular music during the fifties and sixties. Rock 'n' Roll could possibly go down in history as the largest single factor determining the social change of the twentieth Century. Certainly it is the largest single factor in the social emancipation of youth. To say that Leo Fender had any direct hand in the birth of Rock 'n' Roll, is a statement he would doubtless be the first to deny, it is certainly true that the instruments he created were tools for that "revolution". To the historians, he may be as important to those years as Levi Strauss or Sam Philips; one of the catalysts you may say that caused the reaction.

The kids of the Rock 'n' Roll era, of which the author dates himself by including his own youth, were weaned on blue jeans, Elvis Presley, coffee bars, and pink Stratocasters. And the electric bass of course! Without that, the juke box would have been inconceivable!

This book intends to tell the story of the man and his guitars, and the author will apologise for any part of the story he might have missed. To the guitar historian, I hope it will prove a work of reference for dating and identifying rare or old models. To the reader who is just interested in guitars, I hope the story will be another piece of that subject which has such fatal fascination.

Author with 1954 original Precision Bass

FENDER - THE MAN AND HIS STORY

Leo Fender was born on a ranch in the same locality in which he was to build his business and his life, 30 miles South East of central Los Angeles, between Anaheim and Fullerton. The cautious shyness of the man belies his keen business acumen and unique inventiveness.

Whilst he is known to have played saxophone in his school band, and to have taken piano lessons as a child, Fender is not a musician, yet through his talents and creative genius, the whole face of popular music has been affected. During the early twenties, Fender was beginning to dabble in electronics. His school studies included technical subjects like maths and science and he became something of a radio ham. His hobby was to become his living and between 1930 and 1947, he operated a radio repair business and PA hire and service outfit. He had dabbled in guitar construction as early as 1925, being interested in the instrument, although never playing it. His interest was maintained through this period by the odd guitar player who stopped by the workshop to have an amplifier fixed or to experiment with the amplification of a guitar.

During the thirties, Hawaiian music was enjoying considerable popularity, and with it the steel guitar. The Rickenbacker Company in nearby Los Angeles were the first Company to commercially produce an electric steel guitar in 1931, followed by a range of acoustic electrified instruments, and Fender's awareness of the field resulted in his own experiments to develop a better magnetic pick-up.

In the early forties, Leo Fender was employing several repairmen in his busy Company, and was enjoying his experimentation on amplified instruments. More and more musicians were putting pick-ups on acoustic instruments, only to find that feed-back was making it difficult to use any volume on their amplifiers, and Fender began to design a guitar which could not resonate in the body. And so a solid bodied instrument was born! Using a pick-up adapted from a steel guitar, Fender had a solid bodied guitar prototype in 1943, and it was quickly made the subject of the first of many patents. The various prototypes which were made during this period were rented out to musicians, and the word quickly spread that here was an answer to many a guitarist's problem. It was a lean time immediately after World War II, and raw materials were difficult to obtain, and it was still to be some time before a commercial venture to produce the new style instruments could be considered. Much of this early work was a result of Fender's relationship with "Doc" Kauffman, who came to Leo from the Rickenbacker Company, and together with whom Fender was involved producing steel guitars and amplifiers in the K & F Company. Goods like this were in short supply directly after the war, and the workshop business was beginning to have growing pains as demand increased. Early in 1946, the business was poised on expansion and Kauffman pulled out to leave his partner in sole ownership of the renamed Fender Electric Instrument Company which now boasted some fifteen employees, and over three and a half thousand square feet of production space.

In 1947, Leo Fender was perfecting with George Fullerton the Broadcaster, a guitar which was to appear the following year as the first production model solid body guitar. The design was typical of the man - common sense, no frills, easy to build and easy to repair. It was however well designed enough to remain in production to this very day, and by the time it hit the music stores, was as near perfect as it could then be made. The setting up of the machinery was executed to the finest tolerances, and only the best materials were good enough. Experiments with inaccurate fretboards from other manufacturers, led for example to Fender working down his own fret positioning, accurate to 1/1000th of an inch, and then fitting the frets directly into the neck of his new guitar.

The story of that first model, and the others that followed is the subject of this book, but it is true that the activities of Leo Fender in the height of 1948, set the path which rock 'n' roll and all modern musical trends were to tread. He would not claim to be the inventor of the solid guitar; others such as Les Paul or Merle Travis and Paul Bigsby were following similar paths of design experiments during the early years, but Leo Fender is without doubt the father of the solid guitar as we have come to know it. He would doubtless prefer to be known as a practical man rather than a visionary, but no one could have possessed more vision than this man with his new instrument. The competition ignored him and hoped that it was a flash in the pan, but the musicians loved him. At last a practical alternative was available to them, and those amps, covered in herring-bone tweed luggage covering, were to set the back drop of every leading artist's stage line-up in the early days. By 1953 the competition had caught up with his ideas, but Fender's head start found him in a new 20000 square feet Fullerton location, and growing fast.

When the Broadcaster made its debut, Fender was concerned primarily in manufacturing. Don Randall, a radio spares wholesaler assumed a distribution role for the Fender products. In 1953, Fender and Randall formed the Fender Sales Company which was to be the sole distributor for the expanding range. In 1954, Forrest White joined Leo Fender, and eventually took over the production and administrative responsibilities from Leo, allowing him to spend more time in the development of new products, and constant striving for the highest standards. In 1955 some fifty people were employed, yet by the early sixties this had increased one hundred and fifty percent, with a 54000 square foot operation.

During 1964, Leo Fender was suffering from deteriorating health. It was impossible for him to maintain control of the business which was increasing in size so rapidly. Close on five hundred employees were on the payroll, occupying close to 200,000 square feet. And so it was that in January 1965, the giant CBS Corporation purchased the Fender Companies in their entirety for thirteen million dollars. Such trusted colleagues as Forrest White and salesman Tom Walker remained active for a time in the new set-up, as did Don Randall as Vice-President. Fender was retained as a consultant under the terms of the deal, although his new found "retirement" gave him the opportunity to travel and invest in property. Three years after his selling out, he found a doctor who was able to treat and cure his illness, and his insatiable desire to invent and innovate drew him back to the business he loved.

White and Walker left the CBS set-up to pursue their own ideas for amplification design and manufacture, and this original Fender team joined forces to create Music Man, an amplifier and guitar manufacturing Company, which today utilises the designs of Leo Fender through his CLF Research Company.

GENERAL FEATURES AND SERIAL NUMBER INFORMATION

The Fender guitar has been developed around the principle of the bolt-on neck. The various solid, semi-acoustic and acoustic bodied instruments introduced over the years, have incorporated this feature. Fixing was always by a chrome plate and four screws through the body. Latterly three screws have been used in conjunction with a tilt action, adjustable to give string action variations by altering the angle of neck to body. Apart from the 12 string and jazz model headstocks, the machine heads on Fender guitars are mounted on the left-hand side in a straight row of six, or four in the case of the basses. The machine heads have slotted posts to prevent unwanted unwrapping of the strings, and until the end of the sixties/early seventies, were made by the American Kluson Company. String guides are a feature common to all models, allowing the strings to be presented to the nut at the correct angle.

All Fender guitars are fitted with adjustable bridges. In varying forms of differing sophistication, these units are adjustable for string height and intonation, and the original designs for the Telecaster, Precision Bass and Stratocaster, have set the standard for all bridge assemblies produced since.

Until recent years when a humbucking pick-up was developed for some models, all Fender pick-ups have been single coil units. The wiring has tended to be straight-forward with simple controls. Several built-in vibrato units have been developed for various models.

Left-handed versions of Fender models have been available for many years at additional cost, and over the years many finishes have been offered as standard or as optional extras.

All necks and bodies are date stamped at manufacture and can provide accurate age information. The neck is stamped at the bottom end, and must be removed from the body to ascertain the date. The bodies are stamped beneath the scratch plate. but since they are normally sprayed a solid colour, it is often obscured. The serial numbers on all guitars, (except the early Broadcasters. Telecasters and Precision basses which were stamped on the bridges), are stamped on the neck bolt securing plate. This plate has been engraved with a large Fender "F" since the CBS take-over. The serial number sequences are as follows:

1948/49	Three digits etched on bridge plate of Broadcasters
1950/54	Three or four digits stamped on bridge plate of Telecasters and Precision basses
1953/54	Four digits stamped on Stratocaster neck plates
1955/56	Four digits stamped on neck plates of all models
1957/60	Five digits
1960/64	L + five digits
1965/67	Six digits starting at 100,000
1968/69	Six digits starting at 200,000
1970/73	Six digits starting at 300,000
Early 1973/	Six digits starting at 400,000
Late 1973/	Six digits starting at 500,000
Late 1974/	Six digits starting at 600,000
Early 1976/	Six digits starting at 700,000

Old type truss-rod adjustment

New type "bullet" truss-rod adjustment

It can be assumed that the lower the serial number, the older the instrument. For example a guitar with serial number 15942 would certainly be of 1957 vintage, whereas a guitar bearing number 95325 would probably be late 1959 or early 1960.

Up to the early sixties, the decal transfers on the headstocks noted the model in thin black small letters and the Fender logo in silver with black edging. Latterly, the Fender logo has been in solid black with bold black lettering for the model name.

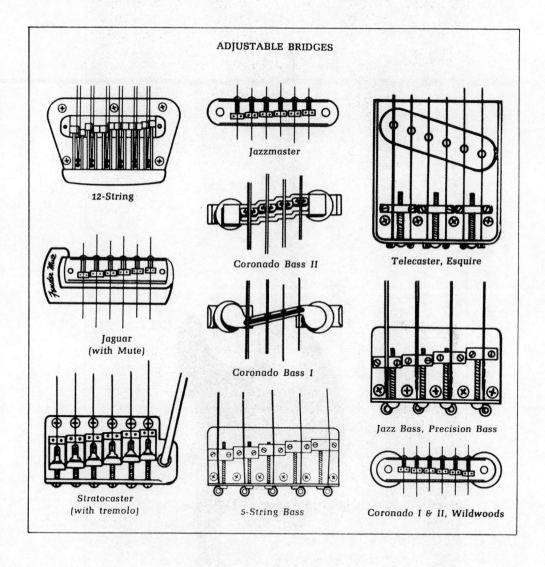

ADJUSTABLE BRIDGES

12-String

Jazzmaster

Jaguar
(with Mute)

Coronado Bass II

Telecaster, Esquire

Coronado Bass I

Stratocaster
(with tremolo)

5-String Bass

Jazz Bass, Precision Bass

Coronado I & II, Wildwoods

1951 Telecaster   Photo: Seymour Duncan

THE TELECASTER AND ESQUIRE

It would be doing nothing but justice to the man to describe Leo Fender as the father of the Electric Solid Body Guitar, and it would be fair to describe the Fender Telecaster as having become the yardstick of success in this field.

During the second World War, Leo Fender worked in his garage workshop as a small time radio repairer. He was building amplifiers for the new breed of guitar players to order, and was fascinated by the response and performance of the electrified guitars his customers were bringing to try out his amps. Although others, notably Les Paul and Paul Bigsby, had been experimenting for themselves with solid body guitar designs, Fender evolved his own ideas as to what an ideal electric instrument might be. There was little need for anything than a "plank" body to carry the hardware for an electric instrument; indeed the acoustic body could be said to be a disadvantage at volumes where feedback would be induced. And so it was that during 1947 with the aid of George Fullerton, the first production design Fender guitar was hand carved, and experimental models were being played by 1948. The design incorporated a simple straight sided neo-cutaway ash body with a detachable maple neck, secured by four fixing screws. A single sided headstock allowed the strings to be brought to the nut in straight pull fashion, and was fitted with Kluson tuning keys. Later Leo Fender had the Kluson Company make his own style keys with a slotted and drilled string post. This allowed the string to be inserted into the end of the post and to be wound through the slot and onto the post preventing string slip and sharp string ends. The original maple neck Fenders had no separate fingerboard, the frets being fitted directly into the neck. The new guitar was called the Broadcaster. The name had been changed by 1950 to Telecaster due to the use of the original name by Gretsch, and the new name reflected the growing popularity of television at that time. However the Broadcaster set the pattern that is almost unchanged up to today's Telecaster - a tribute indeed to the foresight of its creator, and the excellence of its simple design.

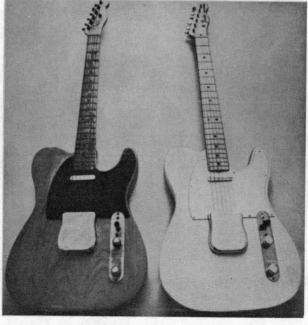

The 1948 Broadcaster   The 1971 Telecaster

1951 Telecaster note serial number 1835 stamped on bridge-plate
Photo: Seymour Duncan

Telecaster Deluxe

Telecaster Thinline (new style)

Telecaster Custom

The new guitar had two pick-ups; a small single coil unit under a chrome cover situated near the end of the neck, and a larger single coil unit set into the bridge/tailpiece assembly plate. This bridge pick-up was set at an angle allowing for a balance to be struck between top and bottom string responses at this treble position. The electrics were wired to a chrome control panel fitted with a rotary volume control, a rotary tone control, and a three-way sliding selector switch. The higher frequencies were especially prominent in the lead position utilising the bridge pick-up, and this cutting treble sound has remained the most popular feature of the guitar. No other guitar can quite recreate the Tele sound, which can easily be distinguished on recordings. The middle position of the selector switch gave a full raunchy lead sound, and the rhythm position gave a slightly lower soft jazz sound. The selector switch fulfilled a dual tone and rhythm/solo function. A black celluloid scratch plate was fitted to the original models, and the ash body was stained to give a creamy limed grain effect, lovingly known as the old Fender 'blonde'. The maple neck was shaped in the traditional pre-war jazz pattern of a "triangulated" cross section, making it easy for the thumb to be used on the bass strings for jazz chording. This feature was retained on this and the other early models up to the end of the fifties when today's rounded neck section was introduced at the demand of the rock 'n' roll players. The very first Broadcasters are known to have been made without truss rods, and today these would be highly valued collectors items, as indeed are all the Broadcasters and early Teles. The Broadcasters and Teles manufactured up to 1954 have specific features distinguishing them from later models. The triangulated necks have the frets fitted directly into the wood, and the serial numbers were stamped into the bridge assembly with the words "Fender Pat. Pending". Later the granted patent numbers were stamped and by the mid-fifties the serial numbers were stamped on the metal plate through which the neck fixing screws held the neck to body. The Broadcaster serial numbers were a maximum of three digits, and up to 1954 the Telecaster numbers were no higher than four figures, although early numbering was not necessarily in date order. A more accurate method of dating (unless the neck has been refinished) is by removing the neck and noting the date marked on the end where it fits on to the body. Originally the necks were dated and initialled by the particular craftsman doing the final shaping before spraying. Later a rubber stamp was used. The pre-1954 models had pole pieces ground flat with the top of the treble pick-up; were fitted with brass string saddles; and had domed chrome control knobs. (Later models had the more hardwearing steel saddles and flat top knobs). The solid black pickguard was originally standard and between 1954 and 1959 the pickguard was non-laminated white. Laminated plastics have been used for the scratch plates since then. After 1954 the treble pick-up poles were balanced for response and stood uneven above the unit. The early ash bodied instruments were lighter than the later painted alder wood bodies.

Shortly after the first few Broadcasters were produced, Fender fitted an adjustable truss rod. This was fitted into a channel gouged along the back of the neck. It was fixed at the headstock end, and adjusted at the end of the neck where it meets the body, by way of a slot head screw bolt. The channel, and the hole in the headstock were filled with a distinctly darker wood, giving a stripe down the back of the neck. At the end of the fifties this method was substituted by the insertion of the rod into the channel gouged from the top of the neck, before the rosewood fingerboards introduced at that time, were glued on. Later in the sixties, maple was reintroduced as a fingerboard material, but this was achieved by a separate fingerboard, not the old method of fitting frets directly into the neck, so the dark stripe did not appear. However in recent years, the old style has been reintroduced, stripes and all.

The bridge assembly of the Telecaster has remained unchanged, save for the substitution of the steel saddles, since the original. A full chrome push-on cover protects the bridge and treble pick-up assembly, but this can be easily removed for muting the strings with the palm of the hand on the bridge. The strings are fed from the rear of the body through six holes drilled in it, and reinforced with metal sleeves which anchor the ball ends. The strings are fed through holes in the plate and over three pairs of saddles, (each saddle takes two strings). The saddles are drilled and threaded in the middle and secured to the end of the plate by a long adjuster screw and spring, enabling them to be moved forwards and backwards for accurate intonation adjustment. On each end of the saddles a small grub screw can be adjusted up and down by an allen key to alter the height of the string. (and thus the action), or the slant of the saddle to adjust the contour of the strings in relation to the camber of the fingerboard.

The original maple fingerboards were inlaid with black dots, in common with all subsequent maple Fender necks. The rosewood fingerboards introduced later had pearloid dots.

In 1954, the Esquire was offered as a single pick-up alternative to the Telecaster. As the body was a stock Telecaster type routed out for the rhythm pick-up underneath the scratch plate, there are few of these models which have not been converted to a Tele specification, although of course the model decal is the giveaway. Like the 1954 Tele, the first Esquires had the newer features and the non-laminated white plate. Between 1957 and the end of the fifties, all Teles and Esquires had a five figure serial number.

The introduction in 1957 of the Jazzmaster, and the following year of the Duo Sonic and Musicmaster, all with rosewood fingerboards, and the more efficient and cost saving method of fitting the truss rod under the fingerboard, caused a change in the whole range in 1959, when all models were offered with rosewood fingerboards only. The Esquire, which was eventually dropped in 1971, was only available from then on in standard form with the new rosewood neck, although the Telecaster was offered with maple fingerboard again by the mid-sixties, and on the Esquire as an extra.

Custom colours were becoming popular at the end of the fifties, and most models were available in standard colours (Fender blonde in the case of the Tele) plus optional colours at greater cost. Custom colours were more commonly seen on other models, but some Teles were made to order in colours, including the Dupont metallic type finishes of more recent years, and the 1969/70 paisley and floral pattern finishes. In 1971, optional custom colours for the Tele were Lake Placid Blue, Sonic Blue, Firemist Gold, Olympic White, Black, Ocean Turquoise,, Firemist Silver, Candy Apple Red and Sunburst!

In 1968 the Company offered a Bigsby vibrato tailpiece Telecaster model plus the kit to make the conversion. This necessitated fitting a new bridge assembly and the separate Bigsby tailpiece unit. A Custom version of the Tele and Esquire were also offered at this time. Finished in sunburst, the bodies were bound round top and bottom edges with white purfling, but in the 1972/3 season, Custom Telecaster was to become a completely different animal. This guitar featured the new tilt neck with bullet rod adjustment. A new truss rod was developed with adjustment at the headstock end by way of an alien key bullet shaped screw bolt. The neck, whilst still detachable, could also be tilted to adjust the relative position of fingerboard with strings for specific playing and action requirements. The new Custom was offered with optional maple fingerboard and optional Bigsby unit. The bridge unit and pick-up were retained from the standard Telecaster, but the rhythm pick-up was one of the new Fender twin coil humbucking style units. The old style Telecaster controls were replaced by the conventional tone and volume controls for each pick-up, plus a three way toggle selector switch. These controls were fitted to the other new model which was introduced at the same time - the Telecaster Deluxe. This guitar took the Custom idea one stage further

Maple Neck Telecaster   Telecaster with Bisgsby   Custom Esquire

Telecaster original Thinline

and offered two humbucking pick-ups. The bridge was a new unit, similar to the Stratocaster non-tremolo unit, and the standard maple fingerboard neck was of the Stratocaster type and headstock styling. To confuse the issue, the Custom was offered in sunburst as standard with optional custom walnut, natural, blond or black finishes, whilst the Deluxe was offered in walnut as standard with optional sunburst, natural, blond or black!

In 1969, the Telecaster Thinline was introduced, having the same electrics as the standard Tele, but utilising a semi-acoustic ash body. A maple neck was fitted as standard, and sunburst, mahogany or custom colours were optional. In 1973, the Telecaster Thinline was fitted with twin humbucking pick-ups as per the Telecaster Deluxe, but retaining the standard controls.

In 1972, the Telecaster was offered with a solid rosewood body. Not many of these very attractive models were made as rosewood became prohibitive in price. They are highly desired by collectors today, and usually feature beautiful graining. They were, by nature of this timber, a very heavy guitar.

Despite all the upgraded Telecaster models, the original design, which is still one of Fender's best sellers, continues virtually unaltered for thirty years, and one must view seriously the possibility that it could remain popular for another thirty years. Tribute indeed to good design and good taste.

Telecaster specification (all types)

Length	38½" (The Tele Deluxe with the Strat headstock is ½" longer)
Width	12¾"
Depth	1¾"
Scale of length	25½"
No. of frets	21

Stratocaster

THE STRATOCASTER

If the Telecaster was the Adam of the commercially produced solid body electric guitar, then the Stratocaster was surely the Eve. Out of these two models, Fender were to produce a whole line of pedigree models. Whilst the Tele was the foundation, the Strat when it appeared in 1954, was the revolution.

The year of 1953 had seen fervent development at the Fender plant in Fullerton as a new guitar was conceived. The Stratocaster was to become a yardstick for modernistic guitar design at the time, and was the first production instrument to feature a fully integral tremolo unit. It was also revolutionary in having three pick-ups, and was the first instrument to feature a contoured body styling.

The Stratocaster's tremolo unit was a giant step forward in this field. Paul Bigsby's design was widely used at the time as an add-on accessory, and whilst the right hand vibrato technique was popular at the time, Bigsby's early units were inclined to send the guitar out of tune, or not return to original pitch after use. The new built-in unit on the Stratocaster was based on a floating bridge, carried on a dense cast block. This block was in turn attached to five hefty springs concealed beneath a plate on the back of the guitar. These springs were adjustable for varying string tensions, and for degrees of resistance to the pull of the unit. A detachable rod arm moved the mechanism up and down, varying the length of the string and thus the pitch of the notes. The strings were fitted, like the Telecaster, through from the back of the body, but the Strat's bridge carried six completely individual saddles, adjustable like the Tele for height and intonation. Whilst most Strats were built with the tremolo unit, a non-tremolo unit model was offered.

The original Stratocaster, like the Tele, was offered with a standard maple neck with the rear channeled truss rod and the triangulated section. The four figure serial numbers were engraved on the neck fixing plate on the rear of the body, and a new style single sided head, somewhat more bulbous than the Telecaster was designed for it. This headstock was however quite narrow, changing in the early sixties to a wider size in the same style. The first Strats were fitted with an anodised aluminium scratch plate which acted as a shield for the wiring, but this was changed soon after to a non-laminated white plastic scratch plate with a foil shield stuck beneath it. After 1959, in common with all Fender models, a laminated plastic was used for the scratch plates.

The Stratocaster had three pick-ups, the neck and middle units being mounted straight, with the bridge pick-up on a skew with the treble end slanted towards the bridge. The units were wired to a three-way switch which selected each pick-up separately. Two tone pots, affecting the middle and neck pick-ups, and a master volume pot were fitted; (the bridge pick-up was tonally pre-set at treble). The jack plug socket was mounted on a recessed chrome plate on the lower face of the body as the Strat had more rounded edges than the Tele. In fact the alder wood body was quite different from the slab features of its sister. The body was dressed away at the top waist on the back, so that it fitted snugly into the player's body and the bottom bout was dressed away on the top to provide a comfortable resting point for the player's right forearm. Two off-set deep cutaways facilitated access to the top frets. A chrome cover was fitted to the bridge, and this was easily detachable for restringing or palm-muting playing styles.

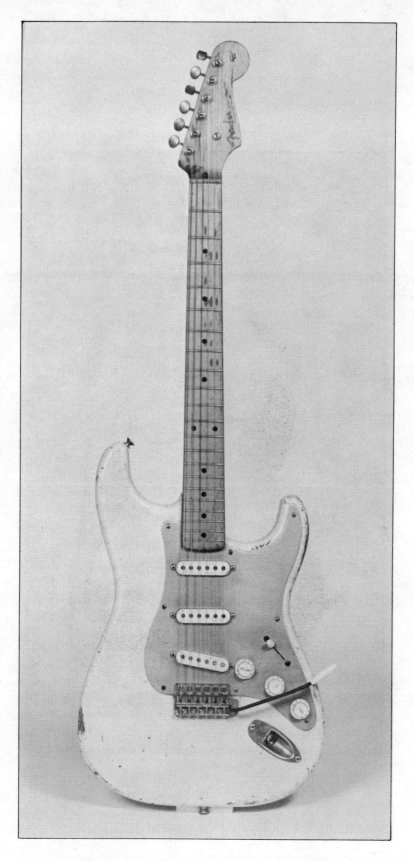

1955 Stratocaster   Photo: Seymour Duncan

Original Fender Stratocaster; *circa* 1958 with original case.

As with the Telecaster, the Strat has survived to this day as one of the most consistently popular solid guitars ever made; like the Tele it is virtually unchanged from its original design, (except for the latest versions incorporating the micro tilt neck and bullet truss rod), and it too has a unique sound of its own, unobtainable from other instruments. The unmistakable "hollow" sound of many Strats, so beloved by blues players, can be achieved by carefully positioning the selector switch half-way between the neck and middle pick-up positions, or half-way between the middle and bridge positions. This provides a kind of out-of-phase sound. All of the older guitars will give this sound, as will most of the new ones.

The original instruments were fitted with the Safety Slot Kluson pegs, but since the latter sixties an enclosed head with the Fender F stamped on the casing has been used on most models.

Originally the fingerboard was offered in a standard 1 5/8" width at the nut, with optional 1½" or 1¾" widths to order, and in 1959 the standard material for the fingerboard was changed to rosewood, maple was later reintroduced as an optional extra. The most common finish for the original instruments was sunburst, and at this time the Fender sunburst was brown and yellow. It was not until 1959 that red was introduced into the Fender sunburst, as it has been to this day. The Telecaster blonde and custom colours were offered but not so common on the older instruments, although in later years custom and Dupont finishes have been commonplace.

Stratocaster specification:

Length	39"
Width	12¾"
Depth	1¾"
Scale length	25½"
No.of Frets	21

Bronco Guitar   Mustang Bass

THE JAZZMASTER AND THE JAGUAR

Fender's success with the Stratocaster was immediate, and during the following three years different ideas were formulated for the next model to come off the Fullerton production line. In 1957 the Jazzmaster was launched. The most striking feature of the instrument at the time was its body styling. The Fender development team figured that if the body of a regular solid guitar were to be 'stretched' at one corner giving an off-set waist, the guitar's centre of gravity would shift, making it more balanced on the strap, and the position of the player's right hand and forearm would fall naturally into the playing position. And so it was that this model was the first with this design. The Jazzmaster's rosewood fingerboard was bound and dot inlaid. Later block inlaid position markers were added (c. 1966), and the guitar featured two large single coil pick-ups mounted under black coloured plastic covers (cream covers were used from 1959). A tone and a volume control were fitted, together with a toggle pick-up selector switch, but a completely separate rhythm circuit was also provided. A tone and volume control were fitted to this circuit, and these were distinguished from the other set by being mounted radio fashion vertically with the knurled knobs exposed through slots in the anodised aluminium scratch-plate. A small slide switch was fitted to enable the lead or rhythm circuit to be engaged. A new built-in "Floating Tremolo" was fitted to the Jazzmaster. Fitted with a detachable arm, unlike the Stratocaster this unit was mounted from the top, and the spring mechanism was very light to the touch. A "Trem-lok" was fitted, and this small button on the unit would lock it solid for string changing, or to prevent the unit sending the guitar out of tune if a string broke. The bridge was also designed to rock, reducing string breakage by the sawing action over the saddles. Adjustable overall for height, the individual saddles were also adjustable for height and intonation. A detachable chrome cover was fitted to the bridge. The Jazzmaster was offered initially with a standard width of fingerboard at the nut and with optional narrower or wider dimensions. Standard finish was sunburst, but custom finishes were available. A laminated shell coloured plastic scratch-plate was added in 1959/60, when plastic knobs substituted the original metal ones.

It was four years later in 1961, that the Jazzmaster was presented with a sister model, the Jaguar. The Jaguar was the most expensive model in the range. It utilised the same successful body as the Jazzmaster, and was again a twin pick-up model. However the pick-ups were of an advanced full range type which were later also used on the six string bass. The scale length of the Jaguar was shorter than the Jazzmaster and the other Fender models, at 24" as opposed to 25½", and utilised 22 frets as opposed to 21. It was a more flexible instrument, and became a firm favourite with the surfing groups of that era.

The volume and tone control of the Jazzmaster were retained, mounted on this model with the jack socket, on a small chrome control panel. The toggle switch was replaced by three slide switches on a chrome escutcheon, being on/off for each pick-up plus a tone pre-set switch. The rhythm circuit of the Jazzmaster

Jaguar

Jazzmaster

was retained, again mounted on a separate chrome control panel. The bridge was fitted with a mute which could be flicked into position underneath the strings for dampened string effects.

Specifications

Length	41"	(Jazzmaster)	40"	(Jaguar)
Width	14"	"	14"	"
Depth	1 5/8"	"	1 5/8"	"
No. of frets	21	"	22	"
Scale length	25½"	"	24"	"

THE OTHER SOLIDS

In 1959, Fender recognised the vast market being untapped by the new rock 'n' roll music, for cheaper instruments on which kids could learn. The floodgate of imported student guitars had not yet opened to the full flood which was to turn the music business upside down in the boom years of the sixties, and Fender were in on the ground floor with two associated models, the Duo Sonic, and the Musicmaster. Made to the same high standards as the other models, the new pair were however made to a price. A slightly off-set double cutaway body styling was used, and the sides were rounded, but not comfort contoured as on the more expensive types. Single coil bar pick-ups were fitted, (slanted towards the bridge at the treble position and encased in black plastic for the white scratch plate of the red or blue finish options, and in white plastic for the shell pattern scratch plate of the white finish option. The Musicmaster was the single pick-up version (the unit being fitted near the end of the neck with a tone and a volume control fitted, together with the jack socket to a chrome control panel). The Duo Sonic had two pick-ups with the same rotary controls, and in addition three position, (rhythm/off/lead), slide switches for each. The plain dot inlaid rosewood fingerboards were available in 22½" or 24" scale versions, and had 21 frets. The single sided head carried six plastic buttoned machines.

In 1966, the Mustang was introduced, identical in specification to the Duo Sonic, with the addition of a built-in floating bridge and tremolo unit. The three paired bridge saddles of the Musicmaster and Duo Sonic were replaced on the Mustang by six individually adjustable types.

The Duo Sonic was phased out in 1970 in favour of the Mustang which was offered from 1969 in Competition colours, having a triple contrasting stripe painted across the lower bout of the instrument.

In 1968 a still cheaper guitar was offered in an even bigger attempt to compete in the lower end of the market. It was to be known as the Bronco, and was offered as a set, with a 5 watt Bronco amp which had the same specifications as the Vibro Champ. The Bronco guitar used the same pick-up as the Musicmaster, but positioned near the bridge. It was fitted, together with tone and volume controls, to a simple white scratch plate. A tremolo unit and floating bridge were standard, as was the red finish, and the 24" scale.

Mustang

1965 Mustang   Photo: Seymour Duncan

Electric 12-string

Competition Mustang

Custom

1965 was the year Fender introduced an electric 12 string model to their range, and this guitar utilised the Jazzmaster/Jaguar style body married to a new 12 string neck. The distinctive headstock on this instrument, and also the acoustic 12 string models, was of a "hockey stick" styling, with a central string guide to permit straight presentation to the nut of the middle strings. The bound rosewood fingerboard was block inlaid, and carried 21 frets. Two split pick-ups were fitted to this guitar, and they were wired to a volume and tone control mounted on a separate control panel, and a four way tone/pick-up selector switch.

The bridge was fitted with twelve individual saddles, each adjustable for intonation. The entire bridge could be raised or lowered for action adjustment, and each saddle was carefully graduated in size to follow the camber of the fingerboard (including the octave string saddles). It was probably one of the best twelve string bridges ever designed, but the demand for electric twelves was short-lived, and the model did not appear in the 1969 price list.

The 12 string neck was fitted to a short lived model known as the Custom which appeared in 1969. This model had an unusual body styling with the bottom sculptured into a point at the strap button. The bound block inlaid neck carried the long 12 string headstock, drilled only for six machines. The same pick-ups and electrics were utilised, and the guitar was only available in sunburst finish. The Mustang style dynamic tremolo and floating bridge unit was fitted to the Custom, which was made in limited numbers, and is now quite rare.

Another rare model produced around this time was the Musiclander, sometimes known as the Fender 'Arrow'. It was basically of Musicmaster specifications, with a pointed arrow shaped single sided headstock, and with the bottom of the body scooped out in similar style to the Guild Thunderbird of that period. Very few of these guitars are known to have been made in a short-lived small production run.

In 1965, Fender were experimenting with a four pick-up guitar. A few experimental models were made, and they were to be known as the Marauder. The four pick-ups were concealed below the scratch plate. The guitar never made it to the production line, and like the Musiclander, is a very rare item.

THE SEMI-ACOUSTIC ELECTRICS AND THE "JAZZERS"

In the mid-sixties, Fender were not only aware of the market trends in flat-top acoustics into which they diversed, but of the popularity of the semi-acoustic thin line electrics. Ever mindful of the need to satisfy any sizable demand, they launched a series of Coronado models in this format, which stayed in the range up to the early seventies, although their success in this field was minimal compared with other makers, and no match for the vast slice of the cake enjoyed by their solids.

The Coronado range was based on a single body styling. Of double equal cut-away design, it was 16 1/8" wide, and 1¾" deep. The idea of marrying the highly successful bolt-on heeless neck to the jumbo acoustics, was also adopted for the Coronado line. At first they were offered in sunburst or cherry red finishes, but custom colours were optional later.

The Coronado I, was a basic single pick-up model, with a single tone and volume control. A new style DeArmond type pick-up was used for this range, and all bodies were bound back and front. A height adjustable cello style bridge was fitted to this economy model. The Coronado II was fitted with twin pick-ups with individual tone and volume controls, and a pick-up selector toggle switch mounted on the lower cutaway. It was also fitted with a bridge top carrying six individual saddles adjustable for height and intonation, and a new style lyre tail-piece. The rosewood fingerboard on this model was bound and block inlaid, and like the other models in the range had 21 frets. The scale length for the guitars were standard at 25½". An optional tremolo tailpiece was available for both six string Coronados.

The Coronado XII was the logical twelve string version, using Fender's newly designed neck, which was bound and block inlaid. Other features on this guitar were similar to the Coronado II. To complete the range a Coronado Bass was produced with a 34" scale and using the famous Fender bass neck in a bound, block inlaid form. A single pick-up with Coronado I electrics was fitted to the first models, but a twin pick-up Bass II version appeared later.

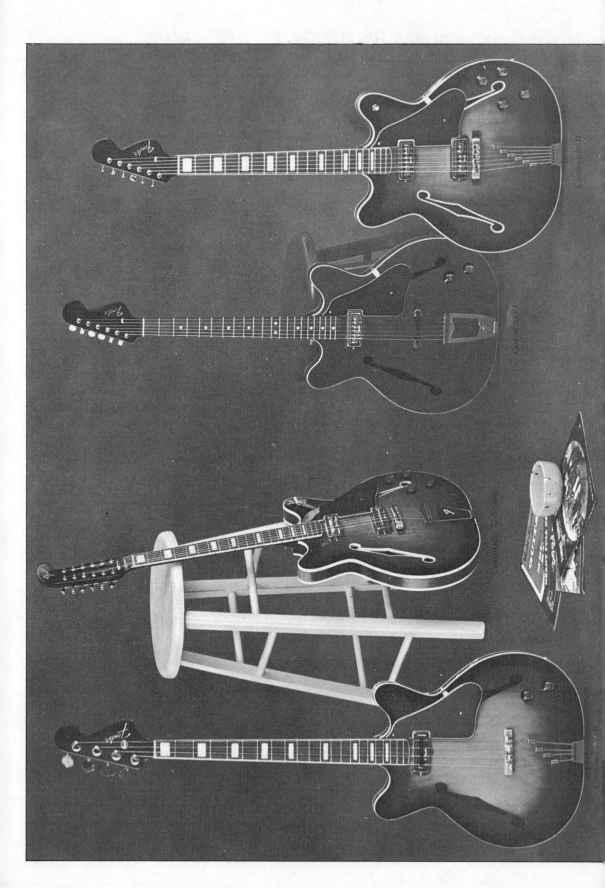

Coronado II

Coronado I

Coronado 12-String

36

Starcaster

Antigua Bass

Antigua XII

Montego II

By 1968, the Wildwood and Antigua finishes described in the flat-top acoustics section were offered on the two pick-up guitar, twelve string version, and two pick-up bass. By the end of the sixties, the range had proved not to be a commercial success, and whilst the Antigua guitar, twelve string and Bass II survived a couple of years into the seventies, the line was discontinued.

In 1969, Fender moved into the prestige jazz acoustic electric market with three new models. The Montego I and Montego II were arched - top single cutaway guitars respectively having one and two pick-ups. The body was constructed from flame maple, with a spruce top, finished in natural or sunburst. The detachable neck was made from rock maple, with an ebony fingerboard, inlaid with pierced block Australian mother of pearl position markers. The headstock was pearl inlaid and bound, and fitted with pearl button Grover Rotomatic machines. The 20 fret neck was of standard 25½" scale, and was fitted with a hand cut ivory nut. A plain rosewood height adjustable bridge was fitted, and a custom tailpiece, with Fender "F" insert. The LTD was the hand carved version of the Montego body styling, and at the time of introduction, was the most expensive commercially available guitar ever. Enjoying the same dimensions as the Montego, (Length 42¾", Width 17" and Depth 5½"), the LTD was an individually made guitar carved from curly maple and spruce. Three heart shaped pearl inlays were set into the headstock of the neck, which was otherwise similar to the Montego. The single specially made pick-up was fitted to float above the carved top, eliminating any resistance to the full acoustic properties of the guitar, and the volume and tone controls were fitted to the floating scratch plate. All hardware was 24 carat gold plated. A custom made ebony bridge was fitted, with an extended foot on the bass side, for maximum tonal balance. The LTD was a late but nevertheless prestigious entry into the realm of high class handmade jazz instruments for Fender, completing the image of the all round manufacturer. The Montego and LTD models were individually made by Roger Rossmeisl, a European luthier of some note, who had been the original luthier for Rickenbacker in the thirties.

The most recent electric guitar to come from Fender has been the Starcaster, a semi-solid model having an off-set thin-line body with a solid centre block to reduce feedback. Twin humbucking pick-ups are fitted, wired to a selector toggle switch, individual tone and volume controls, and a master volume control. A bolt-on maple neck is fitted, and the fully adjustable bridge is similar to the Telecaster Deluxe. The body, which is made from arched maple, is finished in a choice of blonde, walnut, tobacco sunburst, natural, white or black.

THE PRECISION BASS AND THE TELECASTER BASS

With the apparent success of the Broadcaster/Telecaster, 1950 saw Fender start work on an idea for an electric bass. The string bass players were fitting pick-ups to their double basses and coming to Fender for suitable amplifiers in an effort to stay heard in the changing and ever increasing volume of the music of the day. Fender himself, by the introduction of his solid body guitar, had provided the means to get greater volume without feedback for the guitar player which often drowned out the bassist. And so it was that Fender realised the answer may lie in creating a totally new instrument - the bass guitar. In doing so, he undoubtedly altered popular music to the point of laying the foundation of the rock 'n' roll era of the fifties, and all that has followed it.

1966 Slab - bodied maple neck Precision Bass.

Modern Precision Bass with maple neck

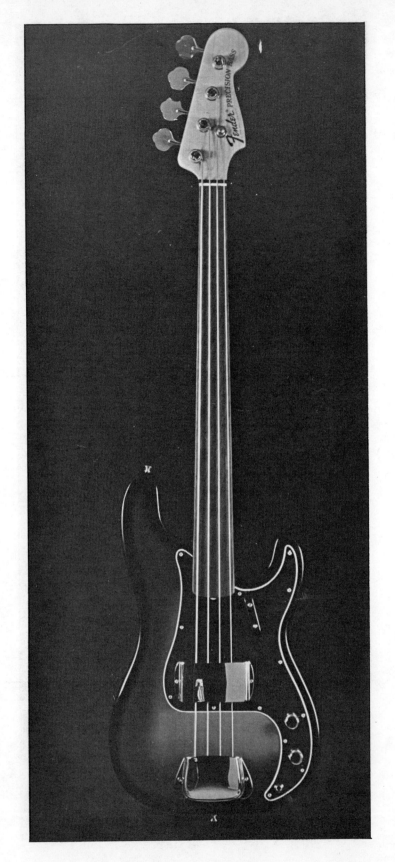

Fretless Precision Bass

The bass guitar was designed with string bass players in mind. It was tuned the same, yet was a sixth its size. It was capable of producing as much volume as an amplifier would provide, and it was fretted so that the bass player could hit his notes with precision. The Precision Bass was born, and everyone fell in love with it! Not only could the bass player put his new instrument in the back seat of his car and sell the truck he needed to cart his bass fiddle around in, but the guitar players realised that with the same tuning one octave lower as the bottom four strings on their guitar, they had something to say about playing a bass line. The revolution was born in 1951, and was so successful that the bass guitar was known as the Fender bass by the Musicians Union, irrespective of the competitors who quickly produced their own bass guitars.

Original Fender Precision Bass

The original Precision Bass came from the success of the Telecaster, so it was no surprise to find that Fender's bass was a big brother in size and design to his guitar. For the first two and a half years, the Precision had a double cutaway style slab body, made like the Telecaster from ash, and finished in the same stained grain cream colour. The scratch-plate was also similar, being made from black celluloid, and the neck design was of the same bolt-on all maple pattern. The headstock was an enlarged version of the Telecaster. A single coil, four pole pick-up was sunk into the body just below the scratch-plate, and this was protected by an angular chrome hand rest, as was the bridge assembly. The pick-up was fed to a chromed control panel with separate tone and volume pots with the raised domed knobs. The bridge assembly was fitted with four individually adjustable saddles for string height and intonation. Giant Kluson double bass machine gears were fitted for tuning. The Precision Bass was simple but effective, and the sound produced fulfilled the rhythm section's requirements, whatever the type of band, by virtue of the very effective tone control.

In 1954, the Precision was face-lifted with features developed for the new Stratocaster. The body was comfort contoured like the Strat, and the brown and yellow original sunburst became a popular finish at this time. The non-laminated plastic was employed in the manufacture of the scratch-plate and a finger rest was screwed to it for thumb style playing. Apart from these cosmetic changes, the Precision remained the same, until 1957, when it assumed the styling it has retained to this day.

In 1957, the single coil pick-up was replaced by a split pick-up staggered so that the half picking up the treble strings was placed just below the half picking up the bass strings. Four poles were fitted to each half, so that the string at rest was in between two poles. The idea was that the vibrating string would be captured in the magnetic field of a polepiece at all times, eliminating the fade of the note as the string vibrated outside the field of a single pole. The new pick up was attached to a new styled scratch plate which also carried the controls and jack socket, whilst the headstock was given the new Stratocaster style shape. Apart from the intro-duction of the laminated plastic scratch plate, and the standard rosewood finger-board in 1959, the Precision is today almost identical to the 1957 model, and still one of the most popular basses on the market. In 1970, a fretless version of the Precision was introduced.

As the sixties swung into the second half, interest was beginning to run high in old instruments, and many manufacturers started to consider re-introducing old features or models. The option of maple necks on many Fender models was a good example of this, and in a hybrid sort of fashion the Company did offer a limited number of maple neck Precisions with the original slab bodies in cream with black scratch plate, but in every aspect except the slab body, they were identical to the post 1957 style. In 1968, however, they went the whole hog, and brought out a bass identical in almost all respects to the first basses, and designated with the name Telecaster Bass. Apart from a non-laminated white pick-guard being fitted, where the original was black, and the addition of a finger rest, the Telecaster Bass was indeed a faithful reproduction. The neck however was a little thicker than the original. In 1972, the Telecaster was fitted with a humbucking pick-up and bullet rod micro tilt neck.

Precision Bass specification

Length	45¾"	(Telecaster Bass 45 5/8")
Width	13"	
Depth	1¾"	
Scale Length	34"	
No.of frets	20	

Telecaster Bass

Telecaster Bass with humbucking pick-up

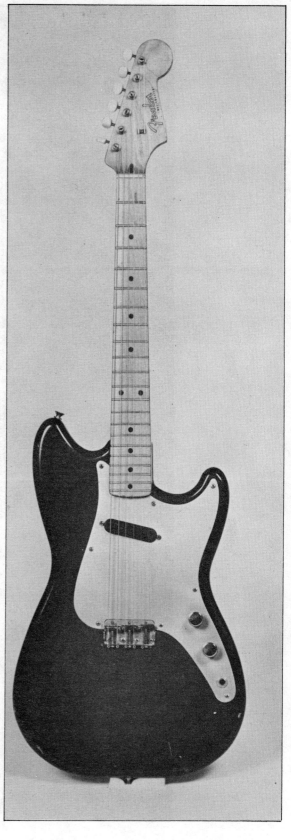

1953 Esquire.   Photo: Seymour Duncan   1957 Musicmaster.

Jazz Bass

THE JAZZ BASS

The popularity of the Precision bass had established the electric bass guitar in popular music inside a decade - a remarkable achievement in so short a period, and it was no surprise when in 1960, Fender offered a new bass model to meet the changing needs of the bassists. Other companies had quickly followed the lead and were offering their own bass guitar models which in some cases offered easier playability and tonal range than the Precision. And so it was that the Jazz bass was developed as a two pick-up alternative to the Precision.

The very first Jazz basses – and very few of them were made in this form - are now very rare. They differ from today's design on two points: the fingerboard was inlaid with pearl dots, and the pick-up controls were of a concentric pattern with one potentiometer housing double concentric knobs, the inner controlling the tone, and the outer controlling the volume. Within a short time the control panel was modified and carried three controls - two volume controls and a master tone control which had a smaller knob distinguishing it from the others. The fingerboard, which was rosewood only initially, was also bound and fitted with pearloid block inlays sometime after. The pick-ups on this new bass retained the Precision feature of using double fixed polepieces for each string, although the unit was housed in a single casing. Each pick-up was spring mounted with adjustment screws each end for raising and lowering the height. The patented idea for eight polepieces was to permit the string's full vibration to be captured in the magnetic field of the double poles. The instantaneous response, and absence of fade resulting from this method had become an important part of the Precision's success which was carried through to the Jazz bass' design.

The Jazz Bass body design borrowed heavily on the success of the earlier Jazzmaster guitar model, and featured the same off-set body styling. The cutaways were not dissimilar to the Precision, but the lower waist of the body was dropped to give a more comfortable playing position for the right hand. The top of the body, like the Precision, was dressed away to provide a comfortable rest for the right forearm. A chrome handrest was placed centrally over the bass pick-up, affording a handrest for plectrum style playing, and protection for the pick-up. The treble unit was also protected under the massive tailpiece cover fitted to this model which also protected the adjustable bridge. Similar to the Precision tailpiece and bridge assembly, this unit had four individual string saddles, adjustable for height at each end and lengthways via a screw and spring for perfect intonation. The neck of the Jazz was of identical scale to the Precision (34") but had a much narrower width at the nut (1½"). The fingerboard had a noticeable taper from this thin nut width, and was especially popular with finger style players who appreciated the diverging string spacings. A normal single sided Fender style headstock carried the four giant Kluson bass viol heads, fitted with safety-slot posts. As in all four string Fender basses, a finger rest was fitted for thumb style playing. Basic colour choice originally was sunburst with custom colours to order. Many of the early models were finished in coral pink.

Jazz Bass specification:

46¼" long
14" wide
1¾" deep
20 frets
34" scale

5-string Bass

Bass VI

THE BASS V AND THE BASS VI

In 1962, Fender launched a six string bass to be known as the Bass VI model. This model fulfilled a demand of that period for instruments of this type: a regular style guitar tuned one octave below normal pitch. In fact some makers produced models with regular guitar scale lengths which necessitated extra thick strings and low tension, but the Bass VI utilised a normal short scale bass length of 30". The styling of this instrument was akin to a stretched Jaguar, having the same off-set body styling, and employing three similar single coil pick-up units. A bank of four slide switches offered on/off for each of the three pick-ups, plus a tonal modification switch, for instant tonal change. Single master volume and tone controls were fitted to the chrome control plate. The fingerboard on this model was bound and block inlaid, and carried a Stratocaster style headstock. 21 frets were standard on this model.

A floating tremolo unit similar in style to the Jaguar, was fitted, together with "Trem-lok" - a device for locking the tremolo unit for restringing or playing in tune with a broken string. The bridge was adjustable overall for height, although individual saddles could be adjusted for intonation. A chrome bridge cover fitting over the strings acted as a hand rest, and a mute was fitted in front of the bridge, which would bring a rubber covered pad up against the under side of the strings, permitting muted notes to be played without using the palm of the right hand. The Bass VI was available until the early seventies when it was dropped through unpopularity.

Bass VI Specifications:

44½" long
14" wide
1 5/8" deep
21 frets
30" scale

The Bass V appeared two years later in 1964 tuned with a fifth C string in the manner of some rarer orchestral basses. It did not make it to the seventies however, as its popularity was limited.

The idea behind the five string electric bass was to offer greater speed and techniques at the lower frets, with five additional notes at the top end. The full 34" scale was retained in this model, which featured a short 15 fret neck (the upper registers being catered for by the fifth string), on an elongated body shape. The bridge, which was placed at the end of the body, had individually adjustable saddles for height and intonation adjustments on all strings. The pick-up was a split unit with a three pole unit for the E, A and D strings, plus a two pole unit set on the bridge side of this to pick-up the G and C strings. A tone and volume control were fitted on the chrome control panel, The headstock was, as might be expected, of extra large size to carry the five large Kluson bass heads and the string guide for accurate presentation of the top three strings to the nut. The rosewood fingerboard was fitted with block inlays.

THE SHORT-SCALE BASSES

One of the prime reasons for the success of the first electric basses was the full 34" scale length which provided such full round body to the instruments' tonal characteristics, whilst retaining the percussive responses only available with reasonable string tension. However, many manufacturers were producing bass guitar models with short scales of 30" or even less, which the new breed of guitar players turned bassists latched on to for their ease of playing and quick actions. And so it was, ever mindful of the musicians' requirements, that Fender launched its first short scale 4 string bass in 1966.

Musicmaster Bass

The Mustang bass was a sister to the Mustang guitar, introduced in the same year, and it shared the same double cutaway slightly off-set body of the six string model. The scale length was set at 30½" on a 19 fret neck, although later the scale was standard at 30". The large headstock and machine keys of the Mustang's big brothers was retained on this model, which like the guitar version was available in red, white or blue. A split style pick-up in the same format as the Precision was fitted to the bass, each single coil section serving one pair of strings. Single tone and volume controls were fitted with the jack socket, to a chrome control plate. A finger rest was fitted as standard, and the bridge was fitted with four individually adjustable saddles for height and intonation. Four individual rubber block mutes were supplied with the original model, but today, as with the other basses, a single rubber strip is supplied which can be pushed beneath the strings, or glued to the inside of the tailpiece covers for dampening, (an effect which bass players use less and less).

The cost of producing the Mustang, to the same high standard of the other basses, resulted in a new bass being introduced in 1970 as an alternative short scale bass for the student, and at the lowest possible price. The Musicmaster Bass was the result, offered in the original Mustang red, white or blue, now that the Mustang Bass had taken on the competition finishes of the guitar equivalent. Using the same body and neck pattern as the Mustang Bass, this newcomer was fitted with a 19 fret neck of 30" scale length. A single coil straight pick-up was fitted, wired on a laminated scratch plate to volume and tone controls. Inexpensive fittings, and basic presentation were the essentials in keeping the Musicmaster's costs down, and the bridge had two saddles, each taking twin strings, but still adjustable for height and intonation. Inexpensive imported machines were fitted to the neck, which was in a plain sanded and sealed finish.

Specifications for Mustang and Musicmaster Basses:

Length	41 7/8"
Width	12¼"
Depth	1½"
Scale length	30"
No. of frets	19

Wildwood

Concert

Kingman

Shenandoah

THE FENDER ACOUSTICS

It was quite natural that the successful Fender Company should turn to the parallel field of acoustic flat-top guitar manufacture in the early sixties. The Fender guitar was by then a market leader, and the name really meant something. It was considered that the bolt-on heel-less Fender neck might conceivably be used in the manufacture of a flat-top jumbo, and this is exactly what was to happen.

In 1963, the Fender Kingman and Concert models were born. Of slightly waisted Dreadnought design, these guitars utilised the same body, although the Kingman was the premium model of the two, available in sunburst or natural maple. Both guitars had a 25½" scale, but the Kingman with 21 frets had a one fret advantage over the Concert. A regular maple bolt-on neck with rosewood fingerboard was standard, and the absence of a heel provided access to higher frets with a great deal of ease. Made for strength and robustness, the Fender acoustics were all on the heavy side, although their sound found favour with many Country and Western artistes. Both the Kingman and Concert featured a fixed pinned bridge, which also carried six individual saddles, adjustable for intonation. The pick-guard was raised from the body providing better resonance of the table, and less likelihood of warping. In 1966, Fender were advertising their more exotic woods, and as well as mahogany, these models were also offered with rosewood, vermillion or zebra wood bodies. By the last years of the decade, the Kingman had been pushed further ahead in the range by the addition of a bound and block inlaid fingerboard.

After a couple of years establishing the Fender flat-top image, the Company expanded the range in 1965 to incorporate five new models. Two of these were twelve string models, using the same "hockey stick" pattern headstock developed for use in both acoustic and electric twelve string instruments. The Shenandoah was the dreadnought twelve stringer based on the Kingman body, sharing that model's scale length and 21 fret configuration. It was finished in natural mahogany with a natural spruce top. The Villager was its smaller sister, being a twelve string version of the new Malibu six string. Both these models were based on a smaller folk style body, although incorporating the main features of the larger models. Both were constructed from mahogany with spruce tops, and both had fixed pinned bridges. In keeping with all the acoustics, both models had a 25½" scale length, and for these two styles a 20 fret fingerboard was standard. The Newporter and Palomino were the two other six string models, designed like the Malibu and Villager for the cheaper end of the market. The Palomino shared the same dreadnought body styling as the Concert, and had the same 20 fret neck pattern. The adjustable bridge was also fitted to this mahogany and spruce bodied instrument. The Newporter was essentially an all mahogany bodied version of the Malibu at the bottom of the range, incorporating however, the general features of all the flat tops.

Later in the sixties, Fender introduced their patented Truss Tension Tube, a tube which ran lengthways down the inside of the body, putting the whole body in tension, and preventing, it was claimed, warpage of the belly. This was fitted as standard to the Kingman, Concert, Shenandoah, Villager and Palomino, and could also be used for mounting Fender's acoustic pick-up designed for placement away from direct contact with the body.

From 1966, Fender offered their famous Wildwood finishes on a flat-top model known simply as the Wildwood Acoustic. Based on the Kingman specifications, this guitar was fitted with a bound, block inlaid neck. The body was constructed from beechwood, specially coloured in the grain during growth, causing the most exotic grain patternings and colours. The backs and sides were bookmatched to provide startling visual effect, and the colour choice was green, gold and brown, gold and purple, dark blue, purple blue and blue green. The varying grain patterns provided, of course, the individuality of each Wildwood instrument.

In 1968 an Antigua finish was offered on the Kingman and the Shenandoah, and this was an antique white finish with a halo shading of dark brown. Pearl buttoned Rotomatic machines were fitted to these models. The following year Fender offered a sunburst choice on all models except the all mahogany Newporter, and introduced their last acoustic model, the Redondo. This was an inexpensive spruce top version of the Newporter.

By 1971, the Wildwood, and Concert models had been dropped, and by 1973 the Company had established an "F" series of acoustics manufactured in Japan, which replaced the American made instruments.

Villager

Palomino

Malibu

Newporter

Dec. 7, 1948.   C. L. FENDER ET AL   2,455,575

PICKUP UNIT FOR INSTRUMENTS

Filed Sept. 26, 1944

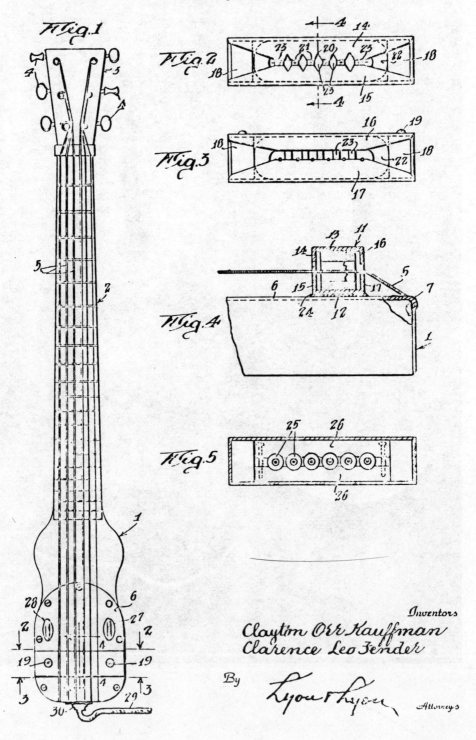

Inventors
Clayton Orr Kauffman
Clarence Leo Fender

By

Attorneys

Oct. 30, 1951

C. L. FENDER
COMBINATION BRIDGE AND PICKUP ASSEMBLY
FOR STRING INSTRUMENTS
Filed Jan. 13, 1950

2,573,254

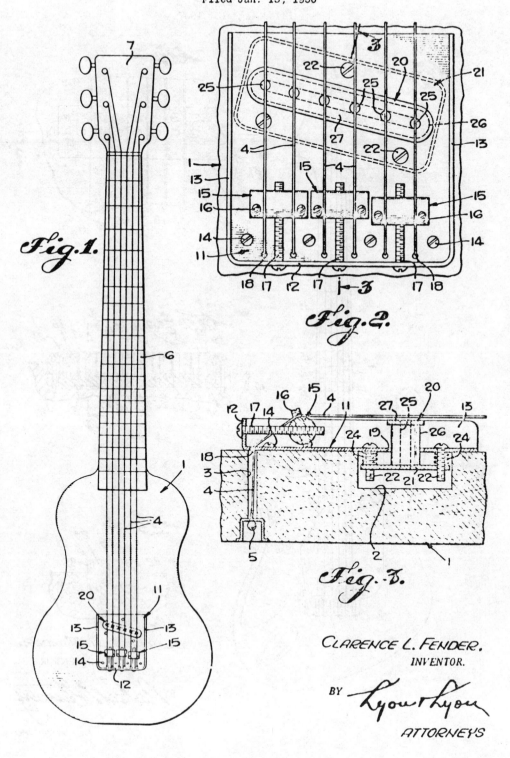

Fig.1.

Fig.2.

Fig.3.

CLARENCE L. FENDER,
INVENTOR.

BY
Lyon + Lyon

ATTORNEYS

Jan. 17, 1961   C. L. FENDER   2,968,204

ELECTROMAGNETIC PICKUP FOR LUTE-TYPE MUSICAL INSTRUMENT

Filed Aug. 13, 1957

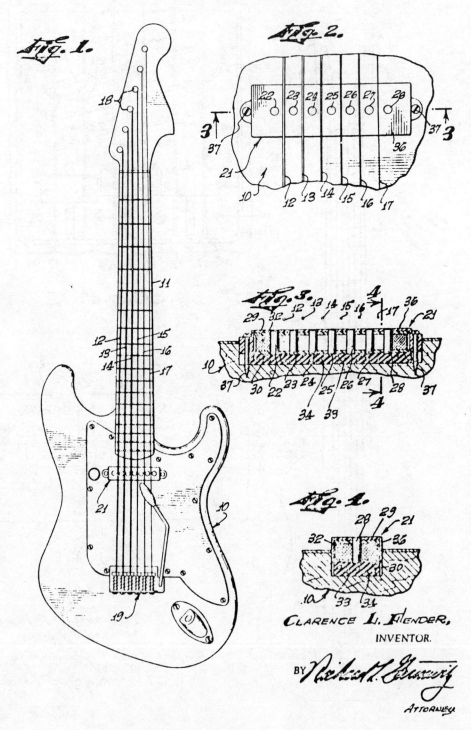

CLARENCE L. FENDER,

INVENTOR.

BY

ATTORNEY

Nov. 22, 1960   C. L. FENDER   2,960,900

GUITAR

Filed Jan. 13, 1958

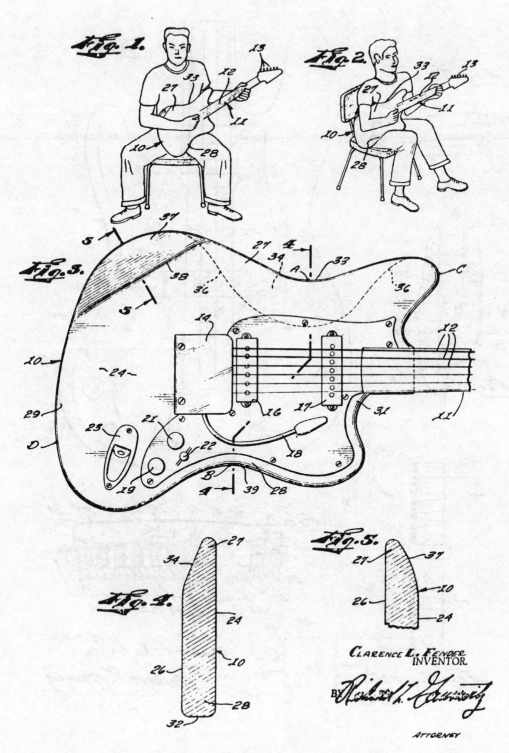

CLARENCE L. FENDER
INVENTOR.

BY

ATTORNEY

March 28, 1961   C. L. FENDER   2,976,755
ELECTROMAGNETIC PICKUP FOR LUTE-TYPE
MUSICAL INSTRUMENT
Filed Jan. 6, 1959

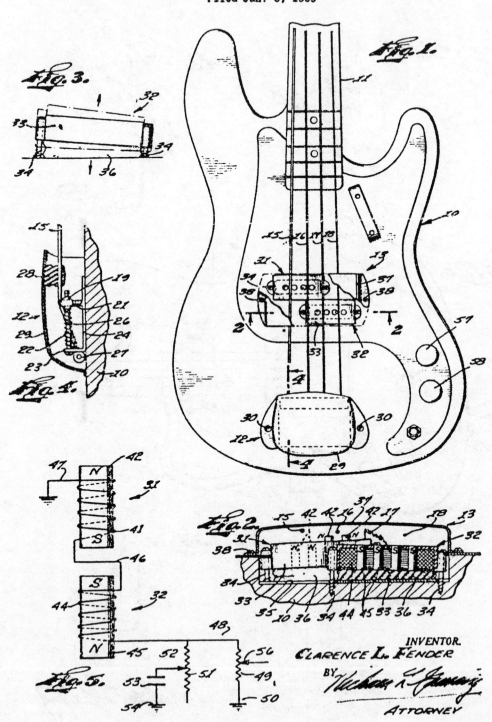

INVENTOR.
CLARENCE L. FENDER
BY
ATTORNEY

PATENTED DEC 29 1970

3,550,496

SHEET 1 OF 2

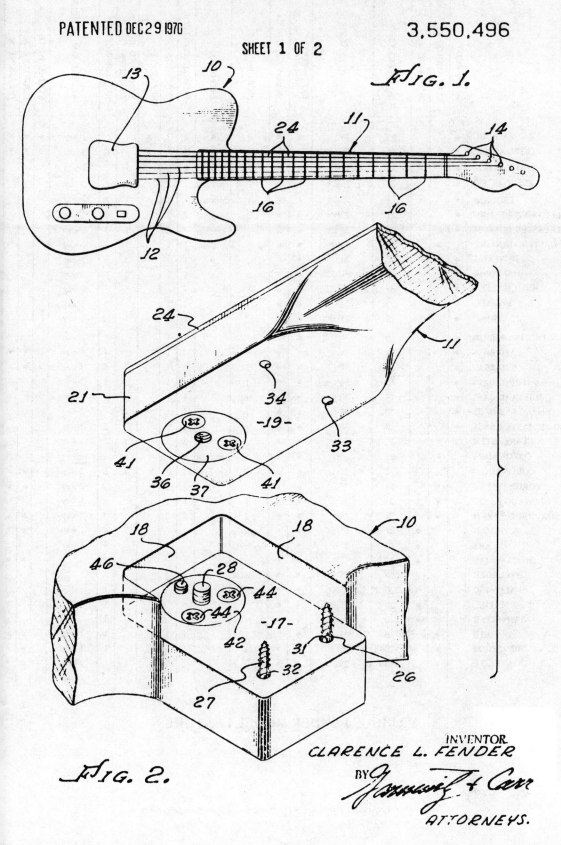

FIG. 1.

FIG. 2.

INVENTOR
CLARENCE L. FENDER
BY
ATTORNEYS.

67

VARIOUS FENDER MODEL FEATURES

	SOLID BODY	SEMI-ACOUSTIC	ACOUSTIC	NO. OF FRETS	STRING LENGTH	TRUSS-ROD REINFORCED NECK	REMOVABLE NECK	PICKUPS	TREMOLO	VOLUME CONTROL	TONE CONTROL	SEPARATE RHYTHM CIRCUIT	TONE AND PICKUP SWITCHES	BRIDGE SECTIONS	BRIDGE ADJUSTMENT	STRING MUTE	BOUND NECK	INLAID NECK
JAGUAR	•			22	24″	•	•	2	•	2	2	•	4	6	3-way	•	•	•
JAZZMASTER	•			21	25½″	•	•	2	•	2	2	•	2	6	3-way		•	•
STRATOCASTER	•			21	25½″	•	•	3	•	1	2		1	6	2-way			
TELECASTER	•			21	25½″	•	•	2	optional	1	1		1	3	2-way			
ESQUIRE	•			21	25½″	•	•	1	optional	1	1		1	3	2-way			
TELECASTER DELUXE	•			21	25½″	•	•	2	optional	2	2		1	6	2-way			
TELECASTER CUSTOM	•			21	25½″	•	•	2	optional	2	2		1	3	2-way			
TELECASTER THINLINE		•		21	25½″	•	•	2	optional	1	1		1	6	2-way			
MUSTANG	•			22	24″	•	•	2	•	1	1		2	3	2-way			
DUO-SONIC	•			22 or 21	24″ or 22½″	•	•	2		1	1		2	3	2-way			
MUSICMASTER	•			22 or 21	24″ or 22½″	•	•	1		1	1			3	2-way			
BRONCO	•			22	24″	•	•	1	•	1	1			6	2-way			
12-STRING	•			21	25½″	•	•	2		1	1		1	12	2-way			
PRECISION BASS	•			20	34″	•	•	1		1	1			4	2-way			
JAZZ BASS	•			20	34″	•	•	2		2	1			4	2-way		•	•
BASS VI	•			21	30″	•	•	3	•	1	1		4	6	3-way	•	•	•
5-STRING BASS	•			15	34″	•	•	1		1	1			5	2-way			
MUSTANG BASS	•			19	30″	•	•	1		1	1			4	2-way			
TELECASTER BASS	•			20	34″	•	•	1		1	1			4	2-way			
MUSICMASTER BASS	•			19	30″	•	•	1		1	1			2	2-way			
STARCASTER		•		22	25½″	•	•	2		3	2		1	6	2-way			
CORONADO I		•		21	25½″	•	•	1	optional	1	1			1	1-way, 2-way- (w/tremolo)			
CORONADO II		•		21	25½″	•	•	2	optional	2	2		1	6	2-way		•	•
CORONADO XII		•		21	25½″	•	•	2		2	2		1	12	2-way		•	•
CORONADO BASS I		•		21	34″	•	•	1		1	1			1	1-way		•	•
CORONADO BASS II		•		21	34″	•	•	2		2	2		1	4	2-way		•	•
KINGMAN			•	21	25½″	•	•	available						4	1-way		•	•
CONCERT			•	20	25½″	•	•	available						4	1-way			
SHENANDOAH			•	21	25½″	•	•	available						1			•	•
VILLAGER			•	20	25½″	•	•	available						1				
PALOMINO			•	20	25½″	•	•	available						1				
MALIBU			•	20	25½″	•	•							1				
NEWPORTER			•	20	25½″	•	•							1				
LTD	•			20	25½″	•	•	1		1	1			1	1-way		•	•
MONTEGO I	•			20	25½″	•	•	1		1	1			1	1-way		•	•
MONTEGO II	•			20	25½″	•	•	2		2	2		1	1	1-way		•	•

Printed in England by West Central Printing Co. Ltd., London and Suffolk